Injured On The Job?

What Your Employer May Not Want You To Know About Workers' Compensation

By Timothy D. McNair, Esq.

ISBN: 978-1-941645-39-0

Design and Published by:

Speakeasy Publications.
73-03 Bell Blvd., #10
Oakland Gardens, NY 11364
www.SpeakeasyMarketingInc.com

888-225-8594

DISCLAIMER

This publication is intended to be informational only. No legal advice is being given, and no attorney-client relationship is intended to be created by reading this material. If you are facing legal issues, whether criminal or civil, seek professional legal counsel to get your questions answered.

McNair Law Offices, PLLC

821 State Street

Erie, PA 16501

(814) 452-0700

www.McNairLaw.com

CLIENT TESTIMONIALS

"Mr. McNair advocated for me on an ADA matter and was quick to respond. He stayed in touch with updates in a timely manner as well. I would highly recommend him to those facing employment issues or labor law questions." **- Julie**

....

"Atty. McNair has represented my wife and I in several legal matters. He has always been straightforward, honest and open with us. The work he has done has been excellent and I will continue to use his services in the future. In addition, I have, and will continue to recommend him to people in need of legal representation." **- Martin**

....

"I've worked with Tim for numerous years and have always been represented in a very professional and competent manner. I feel very comfortable knowing that he will not squander his time or my money billing me for work that was really not required. I also feel comfortable knowing that if Tim thinks the work might be outside his expertise he will advise and recommend other avenues. Highly recommended." **- Gary**

TABLE OF CONTENTS

Attorney Introduction 6

An Overview of Workers' Compensation Claims 8

There are Often Disputes Regarding Who Is or Is Not Considered As An Employee 10

Common Misconceptions Regarding Workers' Compensation Claims 13

Elements that Constitute a Viable Workers' Compensation Claim 17

Is There a Stigma Attached to Attorneys Handling Workers' Compensation Claims 20

The Duties of An Attorney With Regards to A Workers' Compensation Case 23

Timeframe of Resolution for a Workers' Compensation Case 28

Things to Avoid When Involved in a Workers' Compensation Case 30

Accommodation Adjustments in Workers' Compensation Benefits 33

The Factors Involved in Settling the Medical Aspect of the Workers' Compensation Claim 35

Unique Attributes of a Competent Personal Injury Attorney .. 38

There are Often Disputes Regarding Who Is or Is Not Considered As An Employee

In order to receive workers' compensation benefits, you must be an employee. There are often disputes over who is and who is not an employee and there are a lot of rules that need to be considered in that determination.

Some employers want to treat employees as independent contractors, which saves them money on payroll taxes and workers' comp premiums, but there are a set of rules to determine whether or not you're in fact an employee or a contractor. These depend on the extent to which the employer has the right to direct or control the work in terms of when it is done, where the work is done and how it is done in a sliding scale so that in cases where people may be considered or may be called contractors, often times they are actually employees and entitled to benefits.

Generally People Know If They Can be Classified as Employees or Not

Generally, people know. Some people are less clear on it and a lot of times, nobody thinks about it until an issue arises where it makes a difference. If you just go to work everyday and get paid, people don't really worry but if an injury occurs and one is not able to work, then they need to know whether or not they are entitled to benefits.

Typical Scenarios Resulting In Injuries at the Workplace

The most common injury, are low back strains and lower spine injuries incurred by people who do manual labor, they usually happen when they are lifting or twisting. Of course, when you're engaged in physical labor, all of your body parts are exposed to injury. I've handled injuries to pretty much every part of the body that there is, from the brain down to the toes.

The most serious injuries are, brain injuries which can occur in almost any job if there's a slip or fall or something falling, if there's a disregard of safety rules etc.

Fatalities are Covered as a Part of Workers' Compensation

If a worker is fatally injured in the course of employment, their spouse and dependents are entitled to an ongoing benefit. Your children receive benefits until they reach the age of maturity, and the widowed spouse receives benefits until he or she cohabits or remarries.

Common Injuries that People Are Generally Unaware of

There are certain types of injuries that require analysis and proof to determine whether or not they're covered by workers' comp. Some of those would be things like respiratory and allergic conditions. Another issue that comes up frequently is repetitive use or repetitive stress injuries which employers and employer doctors often say are just simply the normal aging process while the claimant's physician sometimes will indicate are due to overuse of a particular body part in a particular job. Those cases are difficult and tricky and require an attorney to know how to approach a case like that in order to get the injured worker workers' compensation benefits to which they are entitled.

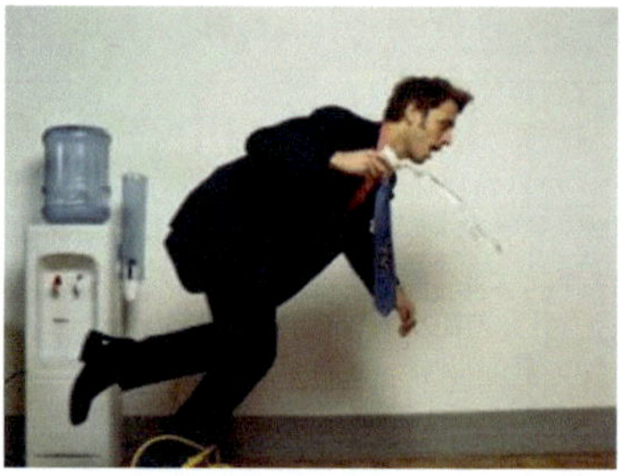

Common Misconceptions Regarding Workers' Compensation Claims

A lot of people think workers' comp is automatic and with some employers, it is. Most employers in fact do the right thing, some employers - or insurance carriers - and I find it varies more depending on the insurance carrier than the employer - will deny or defend pretty much every claim that they get no matter how obvious, in an effort to minimize what they have to pay out. But it's certainly not automatic and generally, when people see me, they've already realized that.

Compensation for Pain and Suffering or Inconvenience is not Covered under Workers' Compensation Laws in Pennsylvania

Often, people believe that they're entitled to some compensation for pain and suffering or inconvenience or loss of future increases in earnings and those are not covered under the workers' comp law. I often tell clients that workers' compensation laws were not necessarily enacted to protect workers; they were also enacted to protect employers from negligence claims by employees for failing to provide a safe place to work.

If An Employee is Entitled to Workers' Compensation, then He or She Cannot Sue their Employer for Negligence

The other thing that a lot of people don't realize about worker's compensation is that if you're entitled to worker's compensation, you cannot sue your employer for negligence unless the employer failed to maintain Workers' Compensation insurance or you can show that they intended that you were injured.

If the employer has no Workers' Compensation Insurance, there is an Uninsured Employers Guaranty Fund that will pay benefits. Claims against uninsured employers must be filed quickly; there are short deadlines. If you also sue your employer, you will have to repay any benefits out of whatever payment you get from the employer itself.

In the case of an intentional injury you have to go through a lawsuit against the employer and get whatever compensation you're entitled to in that case directly from the employer's assets or other insurance they may have.

Medical Causation is One of the Prominent Issues Concerning Workers' Compensation Claims

The workers' comp bar to suit against the employer is, as I mentioned above, a big issue. While injured workers are very quick to draw a causation link between their condition and their job, but medical causation is one of the issues -- medical causation is one of the issues that frequently arise. It comes up in almost every case and especially with low back cases. There are doctors employers send their employees to who will take a look at all of the MRIs, X-rays, studies, medical records and so on and talk to the client and then, they will give an opinion that it's simply what they call a degenerative condition that is from the normal aging process, unrelated to anything g that happened at work, so your attorney has to work up the case properly in order to make sure that there is a good defensible medical opinion on causation before you can expect to prevail. There is often a pretty stark difference of opinion between doctors on that issue.

An Employer Can Try to Force an Injured Employee Receiving Workers' Compensation Benefits Back to Work in a Different Position

Another issue that comes up, is that often people think that because they can't do the job that they were doing when they were injured, they're going to be entitled to workers' comp benefits and don't realize that the employer can try to force them back to work in a different and lower paying job in order to reduce or suspend their benefits, and that's another issue that comes up very frequently. This is a frequent source of litigation in comp cases.

The employer has to prove that your condition has improved and that there is work available to you within your capacities, either by offering the injured worker a lighter duty job, identifying a specific job that the worker fails to apply for in bad faith, or by doing a labor market survey to identify generally available jobs within the worker's physical capacity.

Whenever an insurance company starts down this path, it is essential that the injured worker be represented. This area of the law is complicated and fact-driven, and the attorney has to know the intricacies of the law and be able to develop the facts to preserve the entitlement to benefits.

Elements that Constitute a Viable Workers' Compensation Claim

The cases that are going to be the most viable and least likely to actually require litigation before benefits are awarded are cases where there is a documented or a witnessed incident causing an obvious traumatic injury that everyone would agree is disabling. If you have all of those elements, you're probably going to get a

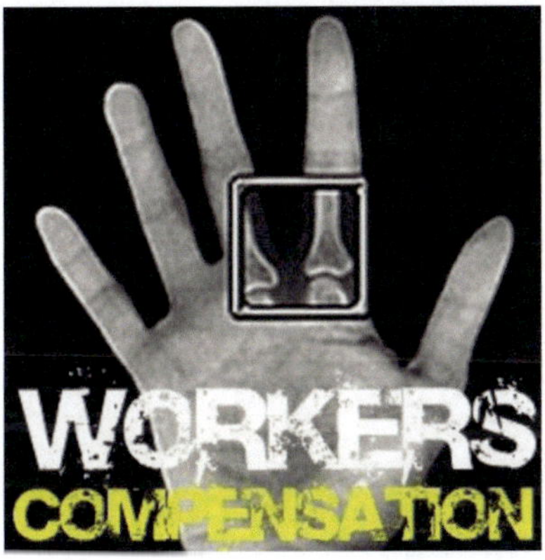

notice of compensation payable rather than a denial. That doesn't mean you don't need an attorney. After benefits are awarded, the insurance company may begin to interfere with your relationship with your doctors by sending a "comp nurse" to your appointments to try to talk the doctor into releasing you back to work before you have healed. It may send you to "independent" doctors to get opinions that you have recovered, or do surveillance on you to document your everyday activities to claim that you really are not hurt. The earlier you retain an attorney the better able you will be to protect yourself from unfair tactics.

It is Imperative to Give Notice of an Injury to an Employer within 90 Days of Occurrence

In cases where there is an injury that is not witnessed by a co-employee or a supervisor or is not promptly reported or involves the gray area of traumatic injury versus degeneration, such as a lot of low back lifting injuries, you're going to be more likely to have to litigate those and prove your entitlement. There are a few things that completely bar you from litigating a workers' comp claim. If you don't give notice to your employer within 90 days of the occurrence, or file a claim petition within 3 years of your injury, your claim will be completely barred.

Typical Mindset of An Injured Employee In Regards to Workers' Compensation

Generally, if a lawyer senses that someone is simply out to get their employer, that's not a case that they're going to be very interested in getting involved in. The majority of people who come to me come to me because they are suffering an injury and a disability that hasn't properly been recognized by their employer.

Disability Decreases the Income and Causes Uncertainty in Terms of Future Employment

With that disability comes of course the decrease in income, medical expenses come along with it if the employer is not paying, there are a lot of questions about their future, when they're going to be able to get back to work, what they're going to be able to do when they do get back to work, whether they'll have a job when they're able to return to work. These issues are generally what is on people's minds and we try to deal with those issues as best we can by giving factual information and analyzing the case to see if we can avoid or minimize the problems or have the claim recognized at an early stage so that those problems are somewhat alleviated.

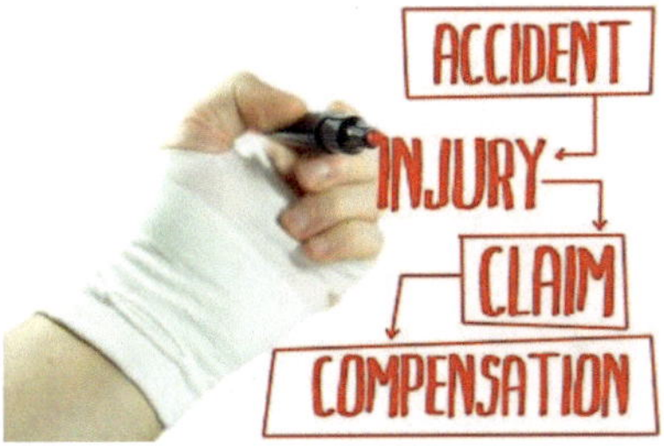

An Attorney is Necessary for a Workers' Compensation Claim Regardless of Pending Litigation

I do see a lot of people who have already been awarded workers' comp benefits who have a serious or ongoing injury or disability or the employer doesn't have work for them. And they come to me because they feel that their right to ongoing benefits is being threatened, the employer is taking actions which are going to lead to an attempt to eliminate or reduce those benefits. And I often say that if you have a workers' comp claim, you need an attorney whether or not there's litigation pending.

Is There a Stigma Attached to Attorneys Handling Workers' Compensation Claims

I don't see too many people who are afraid of attorneys, I guess they don't generally schedule appointments, but I do see people who are afraid to file workers' comp claims because they're afraid of retaliation or losing their job, which does happen sometimes. It is, in Pennsylvania, illegal to terminate someone's employment because they file or threatened to file a workers' comp claim and that is one of the rare instances where the courts recognize so-called wrongful termination. Those concerns are something that we've learned to deal with over the years and make sure that the client knows what their risks are, what the remedies are and what the possibilities are resulting from any particular action the employer might take.

In Pennsylvania, Any Fee Paid for Representation in a Workers' Compensation Case Has to be Approved by a Workers' Compensation Judge.

In Pennsylvania, any fee paid for representation in a workers' compensation matter has to be approved by a workers' compensation judge. People who are getting ongoing benefits, who don't have a petition or litigation pending, will not pay anything until such time as the employer files a petition and tries to reduce or eliminate the client's benefits. I have handled many of these cases to a successful conclusion without getting paid a dime until there is a final settlement. Having the advice of an experienced attorney is a good way to ensure you don't make any mistakes and jeopardize your claim by falling into one of the many traps and pitfalls in this area of the law.

The Maximum Fee that an Attorney is Permitted to Charge in Pennsylvania is 20 % of the Compensation Received

The maximum fee that we're permitted to charge in Pennsylvania is 20 per cent of compensation received.

That can apply to medical bills and to penalties and interest but it would not apply to medical bills unless it was being paid out of the medical provider's share. I don't charge the client for getting their medical bills paid but by the same token, I generally try to get the cooperation of the medical provider.

Most Workers' Compensation Cases Result in a Settlement Where the Employer's Insurance Company Pays a Lump Sum of Money to the Employee

In some cases where benefits have already been awarded, an attorney does get a fee as litigation progresses. Most workers' comp cases result in a settlement where the employer's insurance company pays a lump sum of money to the employee, it's released from its obligations to the employee and the attorney gets paid on a percentage of that, generally 20 per cent. I've found that some of the best cases, for me, are cases where injured workers who are on workers' comp come to me early and I'm available throughout their case to give them advice and steer them away from the traps and pitfalls in the law. I've had cases that went on for a couple of years and the first time the injured worker was in front of the judge was to get approval of the settlement. I haven't been paid before, but if the case is handled properly, it's all made up for at the end.

Most Workers' Compensation Claims End Up Being Litigated in Pennsylvania

Most cases do wind up in some kind of litigation depending on the facts of the case. Sometimes, the employer has a claim that the employee is able to return to some type of work and they should be able to reduce the benefits. Often, an employer will claim that the employee is fully recovered and want to stop paying benefits and medical expenses altogether. Sometimes the insurance company will be denying payment for certain medical treatment or procedures on behalf of the claimant, the employee will have to file a petition to get a Workers' Compensation Judge to order the insurance company to pay for their treatment, but each case is different. Most cases that I'm involved in do involve litigation.

The Duties of An Attorney With Regards to A Workers' Compensation Case

At the initial stage of the case, I need to get complete, clear and accurate information from the client. I have to get the identity of the employer, gather information about the injury and the medical treatment. I have to explain the procedures that the particular case is going to involve and we have to enter into a written fee agreement setting forth how and how much the client will have to pay and how expenses will be handled. In my practice, I usually advance all of the expenses of the workers' compensation claim.

An Attorney Has to Work Closely With Medical Professionals in Order to Generate and Verify Evidence for a Workers' Compensation Claim

In the second phase of the case, I have to gather the medical records and work with the treating doctors to generate evidence or verify the evidence demonstrating the causal relationship between whatever condition is being treated and the employee's employment, and the extent to which the condition is disabling. That is the primary evidence that we have to present in a hearing. Other things that we do are we verify the accuracy of the benefit rate if it's been determined; sometimes the employer tries to chisel the benefit rate down by not reporting all of the employees' earnings or failing to properly calculate past earnings. We often have to take a look at that to make sure that the injured worker is getting paid what they should be getting paid.

In the Litigation Process, an Attorney has to Attend Hearings and Prepare Witnesses to Testify at a Hearing

Once we're in litigation certain petitions and responses have to be prepared and filed. That is done online now. In the past two years, the Bureau of Workers' Compensation instituted an online workers' comp system for filing petitions and other documents. Once you're in litigation, you'll have to prepare for and attend hearings. The attorney has to interview and prepare witnesses to testify at the hearing and then, you need to prepare and present medical testimony typically in the form of a deposition from the treating physician. The depositions require significant preparation. The attorney has to be very familiar with the records and the medical issues so that he can structure the questioning to have the best chance of getting a favorable opinion of the doctor.

The Independent Medical Examination is Often Biased in Favor of the Employers

The next phase is an "independent" medical examination. I don't believe there's anything independent about it. That's where the employer will send you to a friendly physician who will look at the case from the employer's point of view and try to come up with reasons why the claim should be denied or the relief the employer wants should be granted. They also testify typically through deposition and that takes intensive preparation and the attorney has to be prepared to effectively cross-examine the doctor to show that they either don't understand the records or they haven't listened properly to the client. Sometimes, when the insurance doc is one of the regular suspects, the attorney will expose their financial interest in the work that they do for insurance companies. Many of these physicians will make $300,000 to $500,000 a year from testifying for insurance companies and testify that that is 3 to 5 per cent of their practice, which means they are really making some money but I often don't believe them. I think that in a lot of cases, insurance work is the primary thing that they do for living and treating patients is secondary, and the attorney has to be prepared to expose that.

During the Final Phase of the Case a Position Statement or Brief is Prepared to Present to the Judge

In the final phase of the case, we write an argument summarizing the evidence, the applicable law and reasons why the Workers' Compensation Judge should rule in favor of our client. This is called a position statement, a brief or proposed findings of fact and conclusion of law depending on the judge's preference-- those are different formats we present them in. That's filed with the judge; the judge reviews it, eventually makes a decision. Once that decision is made, the next phase of the case may be an appeal. Many Workers' Compensation Judge's decisions get appealed to the Workers' Compensation Appeal Board. After the WCJ decision, there's no new evidence presented. The case is decided based on the evidence that was presented to the WCJ and the Appeals Board decides whether or not there's been any error or if there has to be anything further done in the case. The Board may affirm the WCJ, reverse the decision or remand the case for further fact finding or legal analysis of the evidence. The next appeal is to the Commonwealth Court, a state appeals court.

Approximately 20% of Final Decisions Get Appealed in Pennsylvania

Probably 20 per cent of the final decisions that I'm involved in get appealed by either the employer or by my client. A lot of times, the decision is final. Most cases end in a settlement which is a voluntary agreement which nobody's going to appeal. But a lot of cases that are litigated to decision do get appealed.

Timeframe of Resolution for a Workers' Compensation Case

The length of a case can vary, depending on a lot of different factors. If it is a claim petition, it's going to take a minimum of six to eight months. Sometimes, depending on witness availability and just the speed at which things go it can take a year or more. Other petitions can be a little quicker or just as long. Most petitions involve the same elements. They involve testimony at hearings and medical testimony, as you go through those steps, between coordinating dates and getting dates from witnesses and doctors and so on, it can take a while. It always takes a lot longer than the client wants, whichever side you're on. We do everything that we can do to move the case promptly, take the medical testimony promptly make sure that we're available for hearings; cooperate with the other side in scheduling their witnesses so that we don't get any untoward delays in the disposition.

In a Claim Petition, Often Times People Have No Choice but to Go on Unemployment for a Certain Period of Time

If your workers' comp claim has been denied and you're not totally disabled - even though you may be totally disabled from your work that you were doing when you're injured - some people can find other work more likely than not, they would avail themselves an unemployment compensation. Unemployment is a direct credit against any workers' comp benefits that might be awarded later. But in a claim petition situation, often times people have no choice but to go on unemployment for the period of time that that is allowed. You just have to try to move the case forward. Everybody approaches it differently, some people get help from relatives, friends or family. The attorney is precluded by ethics rules from advancing funds to the client during the case, so while we don't do that, we certainly try to help the client look at the situation and try to figure a way out.

Things to Avoid When Involved in a Workers' Compensation Case

The trickiest situation is where the injured worker is receiving workers' compensation benefits and the employer tries to send them back to work or send them to work in a different job. Some employees, if they're not being represented properly, will reject that out of hand and wind up getting their benefits cut down because the injured worker has to cooperate in good faith in efforts to re-enter the work force. However, a lot of times the jobs that are offered are not appropriate, the person is not trained to do the job or qualified to do the or there is some physical aspect of the job that they're precluded from doing because of their injury. This has to be determined before a petition is filed so that the injured worker doesn't get his or her benefits unfairly or avoidably cut.

An Attorney is Familiar with the Traps and Pitfalls Awaiting an Employee Involved in a Workers' Compensation Claim

A lot of times people get referred to what are called light duty jobs but the job may require standing for long periods of time. And the insurance company doctor will say, “Fine. This person can stand all the time” but if the employee feels they can’t do it, they may not attempt to do the job and wind up behind the eight ball in terms of getting their benefits cut. So, we need to carefully look at these situations and tell the employee how to handle that situation. There are other traps and pitfalls and documents that can be signed or not signed. The employer will, every so often, send out three different forms to the employee, a report of benefits, a report of earnings and a report of changes in physical condition.

If an Employee Neglects to Send in the Report of Benefits, the Report of Earnings or the Report of Changes in Physical Condition their Benefits May be Suspended

A lot of employees may fill out one and send it back but the other two are simply repetitive so they don’t bother. The insurance company can suspend your benefits for not sending those back, so it’s something that the injured worker has to make sure it gets done and we handle that for the employee to make sure that they don’t fall into that trap of having their benefits suspended. Some employees will get a notice to go to a defense medical examination and because it’s out of town or they’re busy that day or whatever, they don’t go; a failure to go can result in benefits getting suspended until the claimant goes to the exam. That's another pitfall that we are very careful to work our clients around.

It is Highly Advisable to Avoid Social Media When Involved in a Workers' Compensation Claim

Social Media is an issue that is coming up more and more frequently. We advise people to avoid talking about their particular situation on a social media because those comments may wind up in the hands of the employer either through some ex-friend who still has access or through a search and some trickery by the insurance company. Some of the most troublesome things are when people put videos or pictures of people, and the big one is dancing at weddings, since employers believe that if you can dance, you can do anything. I don't necessarily agree with that but I do caution people to avoid having videos of them engaged in physical activity of any kind on social media because those are so easy to misinterpret and they can be prejudicial to the case if they are misinterpreted.

Accommodation Adjustments in Workers' Compensation Benefits

There are a few very simple factors that play into the workers' compensation benefit. The indemnity benefit as it's called for wage loss is determined on a formula of between 90 per cent and two-thirds of your earnings up to a maximum, which at this point is about $1,050 per week. No matter how much you were making, that's the most that you can get under workers' compensation.

The Wage that a Person was earning Prior to Injury and the Status of Medical Evidence are the 2 Important Factors in Deciding a Workers' Compensation Claim

For settlement, a lot of factors come into play. The primary one is the wage that the person was earning at the time they were injured and their ongoing benefit rate as well as the status of the medical evidence - who's got the better medical evidence, which side is more likely to be believed - the nature of the injury, the disability that goes along with it and then, other kind of wildcard factors that turn up in a lot of cases and have to be dealt with creatively. The fact is that most people want to get back to work. And if they can arrange to get back to work and settle their workers' comp claim, often they do. And if you have an opportunity that you're going to lose out on if you don't take it, then you have a real motivation to accept less money from your case.

An Attorney Understanding the Psychology of Negotiation is Best Equipped to Handle Workers' Compensation Claims

We have been successfully negotiating settlements by understanding how these factors play against each other and in understanding the psychology of negotiation and how insurance companies view these cases. I don't mind saying that we've gotten some pretty good results in cases that have been referred to us by other attorneys who didn't think they had any significant value. We do our best to maximize the recovery in every case, but every case is different and some cases simply do not have significant value and cannot be settled for top dollar. If you don't have a good case, you're not going to get a lot of money. If you do have a good case, we're going to do whatever we can to get you the full value for it.

An Individual Generally Will Not Get Fully Compensated for His Losses or Damages Due to a Particular Injury

A break even would be good. As I mentioned before, workers' compensation benefits are very limited and there's no way you're going to get a full compensation for the losses and damages that result from a particular injury through workers' comp. What you will get is a number of years of compensation and then, in some cases, ongoing medical benefits; in other cases, the medical benefits are also settled on a lump sum basis and then, the employee is on their own for paying for future medical care. There are a lot of factors involved in settling the medical aspect of the claim involving Medicare and future disability.

The Factors Involved in Settling the Medical Aspect of the Workers' Compensation Claim

Some people who are injured at work become eligible for Social Security Disability benefits. 30 months after the date of the onset of your disability, as determined by the Social Security Administration, you become eligible for Medicare, which is - as everybody knows - is a medical insurance program that will pay for your general medical needs. However, Medicare will not pay for treatment for work injuries that are covered by workers' compensation. That is the responsibility of the workers' compensation insurance companies. So, in order to settle your medical claim, if you are on disability and eligible for Medicare or you're going to become eligible for Medicare, you'll have to set aside a certain amount of money from your settlement to pay for your ongoing treatment for your work injury.

It is Necessary to Acknowledge Medicare's Interest in a Worker's Compensation Case

In some cases, this Workers' Compensation Medicare Set Aside ("WCMSA") has to be approved by the Social Security Administration's Center for Medicare Services ("CMS"). Sometimes that will result in a large number because CMS tends to be pessimistic in terms of how good your recovery is going to be. The insurance company then is faced with funding the set-aside or paying ongoing medical benefits. In a garden variety case where the injury is less serious and a person is not totally disabled to the extent they're entitled to disability benefits, you still must consider Medicare's interest even if you are not Medicare eligible and often times, you set aside some sum of money to cover future medical expenses so that you can remain potentially eligible for Medicare benefits for your work injury if that money is exhausted by paying medical bills.

Third Party Claims in Worker's Compensation Cases Usually Involve a Motor Vehicle Accident Induced Injury

Third party claims are something we do handle; I have a general personal injury practice. Third party claims arise in workers' comp most commonly when there is an employee who is involved in a motor vehicle crash and gets injured as a result of that. At that point, the employee can bring a claim against the negligent third party not the employer and get their recovery that way. The workers' compensation carrier is entitled to subrogation or repayment from whatever recovery the employee gets on that third party claim. And if the employee gets more than what the workers' comp carrier is owed, the insurance company gets a future credit for it. Depending on the case, there are ways of working around this in terms of the settlement of the workers' comp case. Often times, the workers' comp case can settle before the third party claim and you have to deal with a subrogation interest at the time of the settlement. That's subject to negotiation.

Common Examples of Third Party Claims in Workers' Compensation Cases

Besides the motor vehicle, there are slip and fall, trip and fall cases, there are often occurances in construction cases where somebody is injured as a negligence of a third party contractor. Sometimes, people will be injured by defective machine or malfunctioning machine at their workplace, in which case, a claim can be brought against the machine manufacturer. We have pursued those kinds of claims as well.

Unique Attributes of a Competent Personal Injury Attorney

I have been doing these cases for about 33 years, I've handled a significant number of cases and experience, I think, is the most important factor in getting a good outcome on a case from having handled so many cases. The advantages that you have with my office are that we act promptly. We make sure the right paperwork is filed; we make sure that the preparation for the hearings is done. I have terrific staff person who knows what needs to be done and gets it done and is a big help to me in getting these cases. The primary thing is our focus on workers' compensation cases and that our familiarity and experience with the system gives our clients an advantage I think.

Workers' Compensation Cases are a Highly Specialized Area of Law

Workers' Comp requires somebody who has knowledge and experience in the process. Workers' compensation claims are handled in their own administrative court and handled by workers' compensation judge rather than a court judge. There's no jury, the rules of evidence and procedure are different in workers' comp cases than they are in a general civil case, and the law can be quite complicated. Given that there are so many claims and so many different things to fight over, there are a lot of precedents that cut one way or the other, the attorney has to know the law well enough to be able to research it in a particular case and come up with a position that is going to be defensible.

Are Judges Ever Biased in Favor of Either the Claimant or the Employer?

That's a common belief. My experience with workers' compensation judges is that they all want to do the right thing. Some factors seem to be more important to some judges than others and you do have to know your judge. I wouldn't go so far as to say that a particular judge is pro-employer or a pro-claimant. Of all the judges I've been in front of, I've gotten decisions going both ways. Frankly, I have not won all my cases, but it's extremely rare that you get the idea that the judge is prejudiced or biased against your client or for your client. I think overall, it's a fair system but you need to be in the system and you need to attend to it properly to make sure that it works for your client.

Contact Information for McNair Law Offices of Timothy D McNair

My Office can be contacted by telephone at 814-452-0700 or if you're out of town, through the toll free number, which is 800-453-0566. You can go to my website, which is www.mcnairlaw.com and you can contact me through the questionnaire on the website. You can email me at tmcnair@mcnairlaw.com. We respond to all calls within 24 hours.

DISCLAIMER

This publication is intended to be informational only. No legal advice is being given, and no attorney-client relationship is intended to be created by reading this material. If you are facing legal issues, whether criminal or civil, seek professional legal counsel to get your questions answered.

McNair Law Offices, PLLC

Timothy D. McNair

821 State Street

Erie, PA 16501

(814) 452-0700

www.McNairLaw.com

Made in the USA
Monee, IL
05 November 2026

67386581R00026